Rival Riders

'Rival Riders'
An original concept by Clare Helen Welsh
© Clare Helen Welsh 2022

Illustrated by Carissa Harris

Published by MAVERICK ARTS PUBLISHING LTD
Studio 11, City Business Centre, 6 Brighton Road,
Horsham, West Sussex, RH13 5BB
© Maverick Arts Publishing Limited August 2022
+44 (0)1403 256941

A CIP catalogue record for this book is available at the British Library.

ISBN 978-1-84886-907-3

OXFORDSHIRE COUNTY COUNCIL	
3303748852	
Askews & Holts	06-Oct-2022
JF BEGINNER READER	

This book is rated as: Purple Band (Guided Reading)

Rival Riders

By Clare Helen Welsh

Illustrated by Carissa Harris

Gabby loved racing on her sparkly bike. She zoomed up muddy paths and down muddy hills. She was only ten, but she was the fastest rider in her whole family. Everyone in her house loved bikes. Even the baby. Even the dog!

Gabby thought she might be the fastest rider in the whole neighbourhood, but she didn't know for sure. She'd never been in a real race.

One weekend, Gabby's mum asked her to deliver a rucksack of goodies to her grandma and grandad. Gabby put on her hoodie and sparkly helmet, then picked up her bike and protective pads. "I'll be back in no time," she told her mum.

"Hang on – you need to wait for Zac!" Mum said.

"Fine," Gabby sighed.

Zac was her older brother, but he was so slow!

"Hurry up, Zac!"

"I'm coming. Hold on." He grabbed his helmet and hopped onto his bike. He had to pedal hard to catch up with Gabby who was speeding ahead.

On the corner of their grandparents' street, Gabby saw something attached to a lamppost that grabbed her attention. She came to a halt suddenly. It was a race poster.

"A race! And it's today!" she gasped.

"Why don't you enter? You're very fast," Zac said.

Gabby really wanted to enter, but she was nervous. "What if I fall off and everyone laughs at me? What if I don't win?"

"Give it a go! After all, it's not about winning, it's about having fun," Zac encouraged her.

Gabby and Zac went to the skate park to check out the race and the other riders. The route didn't look too bad. It was marked out with string and flags, and went around the skate park, through the woods and back to the start. The race was just about to begin.

Gabby made up her mind and handed the goodies for their grandparents to Zac.

"Good luck!" Zac smiled. "I'll wait here for you."

"Thanks!" Gabby went and put her name down for the race.

As Gabby pulled up at the starting line, another rider skidded over to her. He was wearing a dark hoodie and a helmet with monster teeth on. "Aww! What a cute, sparkly bike!" he said to Gabby. "You don't really think you can win, do you?"

There was no way Gabby was going to let another rider tell her she wasn't good enough to win. "Hey, Monster Boy! If you want a rival, you've got one! I'll show you - my sparkly bike is just as good as yours."

The boy laughed.

An older girl with a whistle put her hand up and shouted, "On your marks, get set... *GO!*"

The race was on. The other riders disappeared in a cloud of dust, but Gabby wasn't going to let that stop her. She pressed down on her pedals and raced along the track.

Gabby overtook her first rider on a corner! She pressed harder. The pedals squeaked beneath her feet.

She overtook another rider!

Things were going well.

But up ahead was Monster Boy. He had just entered the woods. Gabby pushed on harder and harder, faster and faster. She'd never been so fast. The wind was blowing in her face.

All of a sudden, Gabby's front wheel hit a stone on the ground.

She lost control of her bike, skidding across the ground and under the flags, landing with a *THUMP* against a tree stump.

Gabby tried to get back on her bike.

'Maybe I could catch them up?' she thought.

But the chain had come off. She watched the other racers whizz past her.

Except one racer. Her rival, Monster Boy, was headed right for her, riding in the wrong direction.

"Are you hurt?" he asked, stopping beside her.

Gabby shook her head. Tears stung her eyes.

"I'm Jace," he said, holding out his hand to pull Gabby up. Gabby took hold of it.

"I'm Gabby," she sniffed.

Jace showed Gabby how to fix the bike chain. It wasn't long before it was ready to ride again.

"You need to look after your bike if you want to race me!" he smiled.

Gabby was back in the race!

Jace sped away, a trail of dust behind him.

Now her bike chain had been fixed, Gabby was hot on his heels again.

The finish line was just ahead. Everyone was watching and cheering, including Zac and the riders who had already finished.

"I can do this!" Gabby said, gripping the handlebars tightly. "I can beat Jace."

But it wasn't Gabby's day. Jace's wheel crossed the line just a fraction before hers.

"Good race!" said Jace, riding over to Gabby, holding out his hand for a fist bump. "You weren't bad. Although I was right. You didn't beat me." He winked.

Gabby thought for a moment. Even though she had come last *and* she had fallen off, she had enjoyed her first race.

"I'll beat you next time!" she told Jace.

"You're on!" he grinned. "Same time next week?"

"Sure! See you then."

When Gabby and Zac arrived at their grandparents' house, Gabby flopped onto the sofa and glugged down her drink.

"Zac rang and said you'd been in a bike race. How did it go?"

"I didn't win," said Gabby, grinning from ear to ear, "but I had a great time. There was another rider there called Jace. He loves racing as much as me, so we're going to meet up again next week for a rematch…"

Quiz

1. What was Gabby delivering to her grandparents?
a) A letter
b) A rucksack of goodies
c) A birthday present

2. What is Gabby's older brother called?
a) Zac
b) Jack
c) Mac

3. Where did Gabby see the poster for the bike race?
a) On a tree
b) In a shop window
c) On a lamppost

4. What did Gabby call her rival racer?
a) Monster Boy
b) Bike Boy
c) Mean Boy

5. What was wrong with Gabby's bike after the crash?
a) The chain had snapped
b) The chain had come off
c) The wheel had a puncture

Turn over for answers

Book Bands for Guided Reading

The Institute of Education book banding system is a scale of colours that reflects the various levels of reading difficulty. The bands are assigned by taking into account the content, the language style, the layout and phonics. Word, phrase and sentence level work is also taken into consideration.

Maverick Early Readers are a bright, attractive range of books covering the pink to white bands. All of these books have been book banded for guided reading to the industry standard and edited by a leading educational consultant.

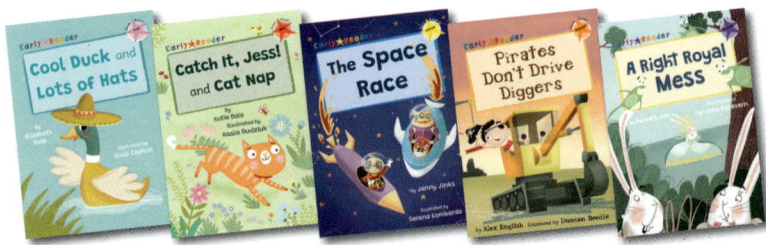

To view the whole Maverick Readers scheme, visit our website at www.maverickearlyreaders.com

Or scan the QR code above to view our scheme instantly!

Quiz Answers: 1b, 2a, 3c, 4a, 5b